The Mystery of the Gold Pen

by Nat Gabriel

illustrated by Jeremie White

Scott Foresman

Editorial Offices: Glenview, Illinois • New York, New York
Sales Offices: Reading, Massachusetts • Duluth, Georgia
Glenview, Illinois • Carrollton, Texas • Menlo Park, California

Ms. Harmony, the school librarian, was one of the most popular people at Tate Middle School. Even when she was telling you to be quiet or push in your chair, she spoke in a voice that made you want to do what she was asking you to do. She was just plain nice. And you don't encounter people like that every day. That's why the news that was flying around school on Monday morning was so upsetting.

"Did you hear about what happened to Ms. Harmony?" Nick asked Beth as she pulled her notebook out of her locker.

"I heard, but I don't believe it. I'm stunned. It just doesn't make sense," Beth said.

"What doesn't make sense?" asked Danny as he joined them and spun the combination dial on his locker.

"Haven't you heard?" said Beth. "Mr. Torp's gold pen disappeared. Then later it ended up on Ms. Harmony's desk."

"Are you kidding?" Danny looked stunned. "How could that happen?"

"Of course she wouldn't take it," said Nick. "The pen just ended up on her desk somehow."

"How do you think it ended up on her desk?" asked Danny.

"I don't know, but I plan to find out," said Beth.

"How are you going to do that?" asked Nick.

"Well, for starters I'm going to go talk to Ms. Harmony and get all the details," said Beth as she headed down the hall toward the library with Nick and Danny following her. They were almost there when whom did they meet? Mr. Douglas, the school principal.

"Where are you going?" he asked.

"To the library," said Beth.

"I know you're quite a scholar, but this is not library time for the sixth grade. Where are you supposed to be right now?" said Mr. Douglas, looking at them over the top of his glasses.

"Science," Danny said, looking distressed.

"Then that's where you should go," said Mr. Douglas.

"But we want to know . . . ," Beth started to say.

"Science. Go!" said Mr. Douglas loudly.

"You're late!" said Mr. Torp as Danny, Nick, and Beth came into the science lab just after the bell rang.

"We're sorry, Mr. Torp," said Beth. "We were going to the library to try to find out. . . ."

"Never mind. You're here now and that's what matters. Please sit down and open your books to page thirty-seven. Look at the chart at the top of the page labeled 'Formulas.' By the way, what is a formula?"

Danny raised his hand.

"Yes, Danny?" said Mr. Torp.

"How do you think your gold pen ended up on Ms. Harmony's desk?" he blurted out.

"The question was—'What is a formula?'" said Mr. Torp.

Beth raised her hand.

"Yes, Beth?" said Mr. Torp.

"Is it possible you forgot that you left your pen in the library by mistake?" Beth asked.

Mr. Torp's eyebrows, which were usually friendly looking and arc-shaped, were lying flat and low down on top of his nose. They looked like two angry caterpillars running into each other. He looked very distressed.

Mr. Torp asked the question again and Nick raised his hand.

"I hope you're going to tell me what a formula is," said Mr. Torp, looking at Nick.

Nick swallowed hard before he spoke.

"A formula is a bunch of symbols that tell you what a compound is made of," said Nick.

Mr. Torp smiled and his eyebrows went back to their regular arc shapes.

"Good, Nick," he said.

The rest of the science class dragged by slowly. Mr. Torp went over many formulas and warned the class that there would be a test on Friday. The only strange moment came when he reached into his pocket and pulled out the gold pen. Nick, Danny, and Beth looked at each other. Mr. Torp looked up, but didn't say anything.

After class, Nick, Beth, and Danny went back to their lockers to get their math textbooks. They talked about stopping by the library for a minute on the way to class. As if he could read their minds, Mr. Douglas was standing by the library door when they got there, so they just walked by.

The three friends sat at a table together in math class. The topic for the day was comparing a sphere to a cone. Each table had a sphere and a cone on it. Nick, Beth, and Danny were working with a large grapefruit and an empty ice-cream cone.

"This is making me hungry," whispered Danny.

"Shh! I'm trying to think," said Beth as she tried to calculate the differences between the two objects and figure out how Mr. Torp's pen had ended up on Ms. Harmony's desk.

After math class Beth had a study period. She went to the library. On the way, she thought about what she wanted to ask Ms. Harmony. For starters, she wanted to know when the pen had disappeared and when it had appeared on her desk.

When Beth came into the library, Ms. Harmony was sitting at her desk as usual, with her nose buried in a book about birds. This one was about crows.

"May I help you with something, Beth?" said a deep voice.

It wasn't Ms. Harmony behind the book at all! It was Mr. Douglas.

"Where's Ms. Harmony?" Beth asked.

"She's not here right now," said Mr. Douglas.

"Will she be back soon?" Beth asked.

"I'm not really sure," said Mr. Douglas. "I'm standing in for her right now."

"Oh," said Beth.

"Are you here to do some research?" asked
Mr. Douglas.

"Research? Oh, yes, I'm doing some research,"
said Beth.

"Well, you'd better get started," he said.

When the bell rang for lunch, Beth ran to the cafeteria to find Danny and Nick.

"I don't know where Ms. Harmony is," said Beth as she put her tray down on the table and slid into a chair.

"Did you look in the library?" asked Danny.

"Yes, but Mr. Douglas says he doesn't know when she'll be back. So I guess we'll have to look for clues without her help," said Beth.

"I overheard something interesting in gym class," said Danny. "Coach Bunch said Mr. Torp left his pen on his desk on Friday morning while he went to the water fountain, and when he came back it was gone. Later he found it on Ms. Harmony's desk in the library."

"Maybe Mr. Torp left it in the library," suggested Beth.

"No, he says he wasn't in there at all last week," said Danny.

"There's got to be an explanation," said Nick.

When lunch was over Danny, Nick, and Beth looked at each other.

"Finally!" said Beth.

"Sixth grade library time," said Nick.

When they got to the library, there was Mr. Douglas sitting at Ms. Harmony's desk. He was still looking at the book about birds.

"We only have forty-five minutes to search for clues," whispered Beth. "So let's get started. Danny, you search the shelves. Nick, you distract Mr. Douglas so I can take a peek at Ms. Harmony's desk, okay?"

"Okay," said Danny and Nick together.

Danny walked up and down the rows of books looking for anything that seemed out of place. The only unusual thing he noticed was a pile of sunflower seeds lying on top of the dictionary by the window.

"I wonder what these are doing here," said Danny.

Meanwhile, Nick was busy trying to distract Mr. Douglas so that Beth could search for clues on Ms. Harmony's desk. He asked Mr. Douglas to help him reach a book on one of the higher shelves.

"How do you like working in the library,
Mr. Douglas? It's an interesting place, isn't it?"
said Nick. Before Mr. Douglas could answer,
a strange noise came from the direction of
Ms. Harmony's desk.

"What was that?" said Mr. Douglas.

"Probably nothing," said Nick.

"I'd better go see," said Mr. Douglas.

"What in the world is going on here?" asked Mr. Douglas.

"Oh, I just spilled these," said Beth as she quickly cleaned up the seeds. "I was passing by and I knocked over this box of seeds that was on Ms. Harmony's desk."

"As soon as you're finished cleaning those up, please sit down and get to work," said Mr. Douglas.

"Okay," said Beth as she scooped up the last seeds.

A few minutes later the three friends were sitting at a table comparing notes on clues they'd uncovered.

"I didn't find out anything," said Nick.

"All I found was a book about crows and some sunflower seeds on the desk," said Beth.

"I found seeds too," said Danny. "They were over by the window."

"That could be important!" said Beth.

"What we need to do is make a chart," said Nick. "We'll list all the things we know so far."

"We know that Ms. Harmony didn't take the pen," said Beth.

"We know that Mr. Torp's pen disappeared from his desk on Friday morning and ended up on Ms. Harmony's desk later that same day," said Nick.

"We know that there were two things on Ms. Harmony's desk. A book about crows and a box of sunflower seeds," said Beth.

"We know there were seeds by the window," said Danny.

Nick wrote those three things on the chart under "THINGS WE KNOW."

"What do gold pens, sunflower seeds, crows, and Ms. Harmony have to do with each other?" asked Nick.

"Well, who eats sunflowers seeds?" asked Danny.

"Some people do," said Nick.

"Yes," said Beth. "But my dad always puts them in our bird feeder."

"Maybe Ms. Harmony was planning to feed the seeds to a bird," said Nick.

"What bird?" said Danny.

"Maybe a crow. She was reading about crows," said Nick.

"Do they like sunflower seeds?" asked Danny.

"Let's make another chart of things we need to find out," said Beth.

"Such as whether crows eat sunflower seeds," said Danny.

"Right, and why Ms. Harmony was reading about crows," said Beth.

THINGS WE KNOW

Mr. Douglas's pen was found in the library.

Ms. Harmony reads books about birds.

There are sunflower seeds under Ms. Harmony's desk.

THINGS WE NEED TO FIND OUT

How did the pen get to the library?

Could a bird have something to do with this mystery?

Why are there seeds under Ms. Harmony's desk?

"Maybe she was planning to get one for a pet," said Nick as he wrote the questions on the new chart.

"We need to do more research," said Beth.

"Research? What is it you want to know?" asked a deep voice.

It was Mr. Douglas again. They'd been so busy talking that they hadn't noticed him standing near the table watching them.

"We want to know something about crows," said Nick.

"I have just the book for you," said Mr. Douglas, and he walked over to Ms. Harmony's desk to get the big book about crows. "Everything you could possibly want to know about these birds is in this book," he said.

"I hope you're right," said Beth.

The three friends sat close together and read silently.

They read about the kinds of nests that crows build and the types of things they like to eat.

"Look! It says they sometimes eat seeds," said Danny. The other two nodded.

They went on to read about what crow's eggs look like and how they keep their feathers clean. Then they came upon a chapter about the unusual habits of crows.

"Wow! Listen to this," cried Beth. She read aloud in an excited whisper to the boys. "Crows are attracted to shiny objects and have been known to swoop down and carry off such things as coins, rings, and other items of value."

"Like gold pens!" shouted Danny.

"Wait, there's more," said Beth. "Crows can become quite tame, and these shiny objects sometimes serve as thank-you gifts which they give to people who feed them."

"That's it!" cried Nick.

"The gold pen must have been a thank-you gift from some crow Ms. Harmony's been feeding," said Danny.

"We've got to find that crow," said Beth.

Just then the bell rang and library period was over.

"Let's meet in the library after school and solve this mystery once and for all," said Nick.

After the final bell rang, Beth hurried to the library where Danny and Nick were already waiting.

"What are we going to do now?" she asked.

"Let's find the crow," said Nick.

"How?" asked Danny.

"Where exactly did you find those seeds?" asked Beth.

"Come on, I'll show you," said Danny as he led them over to the window.

Mr. Douglas was over near the window putting some books away.

"Back so soon?" he asked.

"We have a little more research to do," said Beth.

Just then they heard a tapping sound and looked up to see a large crow sitting on the windowsill pecking at the window.

"Look!" cried Beth. "There's our crow!"

"Your crow?" asked Mr. Douglas.

"Actually, it's Ms. Harmony's crow," said Nick.

Nick, Beth, and Danny explained the whole thing about the crow and the seeds and the shiny objects to Mr. Douglas.

"That's amazing," he said, "but we still don't have any real proof that the crow took the pen."

"We have to get him to do it again," said Danny.

"Let's go talk to Mr. Torp," said Beth.

Off they went to find Mr. Torp and explain about the crow.

"All we have to do is get the crow to take your pen again and the mystery will be solved," said Beth as she poured out the story to Mr. Torp a few minutes later.

"It's worth a try," said Mr. Torp. "Nick, open that window and Danny, you go open the library window. Now, I'll put my pen here on the desk and let's cross our fingers and wait."

"We'd better hide somewhere or the crow might not come in," said Beth.

"Good point," said Mr. Torp. "Let's wait in the hall. We can watch through the window in the door."

They all went out in the hall and waited for the crow to come. They waited a long time, but just when they were about to give up they heard a loud "CAW." The crow flew in the window, picked up the pen in its beak, and flew back out.

"Quick! Let's go to the library!" cried Beth.

Just as they hoped, when they got to the library, there was the crow, sitting on Ms. Harmony's desk with the gold pen still in its beak.

"It worked!" shouted Nick.

"It certainly did," said a soft familiar voice.

"Ms. Harmony!" cried Beth.

"Don't get too close, Beth. I have a cold. That's why I wasn't in school today. Mr. Douglas called me and told me about your plan. Even though I'm under the weather, I just had to come and see if it would work," she said.

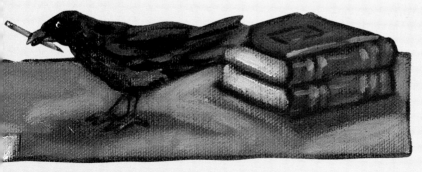

"You kids solved the mystery," said Mr. Torp. "I just couldn't figure out how my pen had ended up in the library."

"Now we know it flew here!" said Mr. Douglas.

Everyone laughed.

"Well, George, you certainly had us wondering," said Ms. Harmony.

"George?" said Beth.

"Yes, meet my generous friend, George," said Ms. Harmony, pointing to the crow.

"I think we should give George some sunflower seeds to thank him for helping us solve the mystery," said Danny.

"That's a good idea, Danny, but be careful. If you feed him, he may end up trying to give you something shiny in return," said Ms. Harmony.

"I could use a new watch," said Danny.

Ms. Harmony laughed and bent down close to the crow.

"He was only kidding, George," she whispered.